NEED TO KNOW for

NEW PARENTS

JEFF ATWOOD

HARVEST HOUSE PUBLISHERS
EUGENE, OREGON

Cover and interior design by Studio Gearbox
Cover photo © DandelionFly / Shutterstock

Published in partnership with Brentwood Studios.
BrentwoodStudios.net

Need to Know for New Parents
Copyright © 2020 by Jeff Atwood
Published by Harvest House Publishers
Eugene, Oregon 97408
www.harvesthousepublishers.com

ISBN 978-0-7369-8113-2 (hardcover)
ISBN 978-0-7369-8114-9 (ebook)

Printed in the United States of America

20 21 22 23 24 25 26 27 28 / VP / 10 9 8 7 6 5 4 3 2 1

TO MADISON, MCKENZIE,
AND MACIE—
THANKS FOR MAKING
ME A DAD.

INTRODUCTION

Congratulations! Being a parent is an amazing thing. You get the honor/challenge/thrill/desperation (those feelings change minute by minute) of shaping the life of another amazingly, miraculously created human being. Parenting will take every bit of your strength (and more) every day but will reward you in ways you could never have imagined. My wife and I raised three daughters, and every word on the pages that follow is born out of our experiences—both good and bad.

I wish you all the best as you enter this amazing new chapter of life.

Special thanks to Holly and Chris Kowalski, Adrienne and Jay Williams, Leslianna and Andy Garlington, and Melissa and Carter Watkins (great parents all) for their review and input on early versions of this book.

MY "NEED TO KNOW"

If you are giving this book as a gift to the parents of a newborn, you are aware that they need to know a lot more than what is contained in these pages. Please take a minute to share advice you think the recipients of this book need to know about parenting.

The same applies to you, the reader. Please take a moment to write down some ideas or experiences you want to remember so you can share them with other new parents.

TELL YOUR SPOUSE
"I LOVE YOU"
A LOT DURING THE DAY.
FILL THAT LOVE TANK TO THE BRIM
TO COUNTERACT
THE SNIPPINESS
THAT CAN OCCUR DURING THE
1:00 A.M., 2:15 A.M., 3:28 A.M.,
3:46 A.M., AND 5:11 A.M.
FEEDINGS, CRYING, DIRTY DIAPERS,
AND GENERAL BABY FUSSINESS.

NEVER GO HALFWAY WITH A HUG.

WHEN YOUR CHILD LEANS INTO YOU,

BE 100% COMMITED TO THE HUG

FOR 100% OF THE HUG'S DURATION.

BABY MATH IS SIMPLE.

JUST TAKE THE REASONABLY EXPECTED AMOUNT OF

TIME NEEDED TO COMPLETE A SIMPLE TASK

AND MULTIPLY THAT BY INFINITY.

THEN ADD 15 MINUTES.

THERE ARE NEARLY AS MANY
"LASTS" AS "FIRSTS" WITH BABIES.
"FIRSTS" ARE LIKE FIREWORKS.
BIG, BRIGHT, AND NOISY.
"LASTS" ARE QUIETER
AND EASILY OVERLOOKED.
THE FIRST STEP ULTIMATELY MEANS THE LAST CRAWL.

THE FIRST BITE OF SOLID FOOD SIGNALS

THE LAST BOTTLE OR THE END OF NURSING.
WATCH FOR THE "LASTS"
AND CELEBRATE THEM TOO.

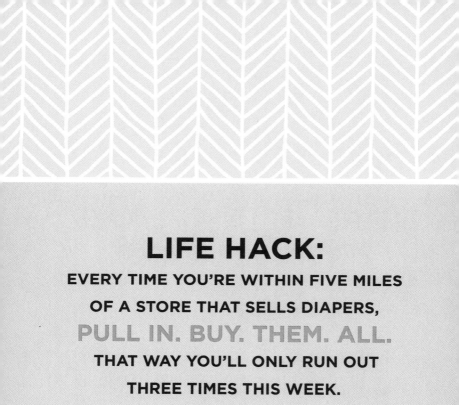

LIFE HACK:

EVERY TIME YOU'RE WITHIN FIVE MILES
OF A STORE THAT SELLS DIAPERS,
PULL IN. BUY. THEM. ALL.
THAT WAY YOU'LL ONLY RUN OUT
THREE TIMES THIS WEEK.

KIDS NEED LESS STUFF THAN YOU THINK.

THEY MAY LIKE THE $100 GIZMO YOU BOUGHT THEM, BUT THERE'S A PRETTY GOOD CHANCE THEY'LL BE EVEN MORE EXCITED ABOUT THE BOX IT CAME IN.

WHEN YOUR KID MOANS,
"WHY DO I HAVE TO?"
SAYING "BECAUSE I'M THE MOM (OR DAD)"
IS THE VERBAL EQUIVALENT OF A FIRE EXTINGUISHER.
BRING IT OUT ONLY IN AN EMERGENCY.
IT MAY GET THE JOB DONE,
BUT YOU ARE OFTEN LEFT WITH A HORRIBLE MESS.

EVERYTHING WITH KIDS IS A PHASE.
IF IT'S A GOOD PHASE,
TREASURE IT.
IF IT'S A BAD PHASE,
TAKE COMFORT KNOWING
IT WILL SOON BE OVER.

APPROXIMATELY 97.8% OF PARENTS LIE ABOUT THEIR KIDS' SUPPOSED AWESOMENESS.

HERE'S THE THING: YOU'VE SEEN THEIR KIDS.

THEY'RE NOT REALLY THAT AWESOME.

DON'T GET SUCKED INTO THE COMPARISON GAME.

BE VERY CAREFUL ABOUT CONFUSING

A FILLED-UP CALENDAR

WITH A FULFILLING LIFE.

KIDS NEED SPACE TO

JUST BE KIDS.

THERE'S NO SHAME IN EATING CEREAL FOR DINNER EVERY NIGHT.

YOU'VE GOT LIMITED NATURAL RESOURCES (TIME AND ENERGY).

YOU MUST PRIORITIZE AND CONSERVE THOSE RESOURCES FOR IMPORTANT PARENTING STUFF.

MAKING DINNER IS OPTIONAL.

CLEANING VOMIT IS NOT.

YES, CHILDREN ARE SELFISH.
BUT HAVE COMPASSION—
THEY LIKELY LEARNED
IT FROM YOU.

BE CAREFUL ABOUT CHASING THINGS
TOO HARD AND TOO EARLY.
IT'S HIGHLY UNLIKELY THAT ANYONE
HAS TOLD THEIR PARENTS,
**"I WOULD HAVE BEEN
MORE SUCCESSFUL IN LIFE
IF YOU HAD LET ME PLAY
ON THAT THREE-YEAR-OLD
TRAVEL SOCCER TEAM."**

TRUST YOUR INSTINCTS.

GOD GAVE YOU EVERYTHING YOU
NEED TO BE A GOOD PARENT.
YOU HAVE IT IN YOU.
YOU JUST NEED TO TRUST THAT YOU DO.

THE SMELL OF A
FRESHLY BATHED NEWBORN
IS INTOXICATING.
SOAK IT UP AND
REMEMBER IT FOREVER.

THERE IS NO PERFECT WAY TO CHANGE A DIAPER.

IT'S OKAY IF YOUR
SPOUSE, PARENT, OR IN-LAW
DOES IT A LITTLE DIFFERENTLY
THAN YOU DO.

IT'S ONLY FAIR

YOU TRY THE BABY FOOD YOURSELF
BEFORE YOU FEED
IT TO YOUR CHILD.

IF PARENTS HAVE
A SUPERPOWER,
IT IS BURPING THE BABY.
YOU CAN MIRACULOUSLY
TRANSFORM A SITUATION
JUST BY PATTING SOMEONE'S BACK.

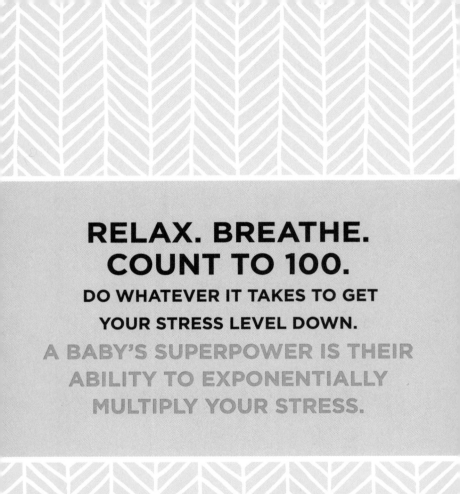

RELAX. BREATHE. COUNT TO 100.

DO WHATEVER IT TAKES TO GET YOUR STRESS LEVEL DOWN.

A BABY'S SUPERPOWER IS THEIR ABILITY TO EXPONENTIALLY MULTIPLY YOUR STRESS.

HOLDING YOUR NEWBORN FOR THE FIRST TIME IS LIKE

DANCING TO A SLOW SONG AT THE MIDDLE SCHOOL DANCE.

1: YOU'RE EXCITED AND NAUSEOUS AT THE SAME TIME.

2: "WHERE DO I PUT MY HANDS?"

3: YOU'RE TRYING TO FIND YOUR BALANCE WHILE YOUR HEART IS RACING.

4: "THIS IS *REALLY NICE*."

5: YOUR BABY OR YOUR DANCE PARTNER THROWS UP ON YOUR SHOES.

DON'T EVER SAY
"WE WON'T BE *THOSE PARENTS*."
AT SOME POINT, WE ARE ALL
THOSE PARENTS.

CHILD DEVELOPMENT
IS NOT A RACE.
THERE'S NO BLUE RIBBON
OR TROPHY
FOR HAVING THE KID WHO DOES
SOMETHING BEFORE THE OTHER KIDS.

FAKE SLEEPING

**WHILE THE BABY CRIES AT 3:00 A.M.
SO YOUR SPOUSE WILL GET UP
IS A REAL THING.**

(BUT NOT A GOOD THING.)

YOU WILL NOT BE
THE FIRST OR LAST PARENT
TO FALL ASLEEP IN THE SHOWER.
OR AT THE KITCHEN TABLE.
OR READING BEDTIME STORIES.
NEWBORN SLEEP DEPRIVATION IS SIMPLY
BOOT CAMP FOR THE TEENAGE YEARS.

STARING AT YOUR BABY IS GOOD. HE OR SHE IS A MAGNIFICENT, AMAZING, MIRACULOUS CREATION. **IT'S OKAY TO GAWK.**

HELP YOUR KIDS FIND
WHAT BRINGS THEM JOY,
NOT JUST WHAT YOU ENJOY.
LEARN ABOUT THEIR INTERESTS AND INVEST IN THEM.
INTERESTS BECOME HOBBIES
THAT CAN UNLEASH PASSIONS.

USE GOOFY CHARACTER VOICES
WHEN READING BOOKS.
YOUR SON WON'T REMEMBER THE BOOK,
BUT HE WILL REMEMBER
HOW YOU SOUNDED LIKE
"BOBBY THE BAD, BAD BILLY GOAT"
WAS TALKING INTO A
FAN-NUH-NIH-NIH-NIH-NUH.

EMBRACE THE MESS

THAT COMES WHEN YOU SUDDENLY HAVE
50% MORE PEOPLE IN YOUR HOME.
DON'T HIDE IT. DON'T COVER IT UP.
DON'T APOLOGIZE FOR IT WHEN
PEOPLE COME SEE THE BABY.
THERE IS NOTHING ORDERLY OR
ORGANIZED ABOUT HAVING A NEWBORN.

GIVE YOUR SPOUSE
A SURPRISE BREAK.
IT'S AMAZING HOW AN
UNEXPECTED 30 FREE MINUTES
CHANGES THINGS.

BREAKING NEWS:
YOU ARE NOT
THE FIRST PARENTS TO
BE SCARED TO DEATH
ABOUT BEING PARENTS.

YOU OFTEN SEE
BABY FOOD TWICE.
(THIS IS MORE A WARNING
THAN AN OBSERVATION.)

DON'T MISS THE BEST MOMENTS
TRYING TO MAKE MEMORIES.

NOT EVERYTHING HAS TO BE
BIGGER AND BRIGHTER AND BETTER
THAN THE GIRL ON PINTEREST WITH
THE COLOR-COORDINATED TOY TUBS.

KEEP IT SIMPLE.

MEMORIES WILL MAKE THEMSELVES.

IF ANYONE BUT
A COMPLETE STRANGER
OR A JERRY SPRINGER SHOW
GUEST SAYS,
"LET ME KEEP THE BABY
FOR THE AFTERNOON,"
LET THEM.

SUCCESSFUL PARENTING
IS 49% GOOD PLANNING
AND 51% RESPONDING
TO THE CHALLENGE OF THE MOMENT.

NO MATTER THE
BOOKS YOU'VE READ,
THE CLASSES YOU'VE TAKEN,
OR WHAT YOUR FRIENDS MIGHT SAY,
THERE REALLY IS NO SUBSTITUTE
FOR BABY-RAISING
ADVICE FROM GRANDMA.

BREAD CRUST IS NOT A CARCINOGEN.

LIL' SPARKY OR SISSY CAN EAT IT ALL AND BE JUST FINE.

NO MATTER WHAT YOU DO OR SAY OR BOUNCE OR PRAY, SOMETIMES BABIES JUST CRY.

THEY JUST DO. THEY'RE BABIES.

KEEP ALL THE PICTURES

(GOOD AND BAD) ON YOUR PHONE.

IT BRINGS BALANCE TO EXPECTATIONS.

NEVER LIE ON THE FLOOR AND DO THE
"HEY, LOOK—THE BABY IS AN AIRPLANE"
THING WITH A WIDE-OPEN MOUTH.
ALL FLUIDS FOLLOW THE LAW OF GRAVITY.

GIVE YOURSELF THE SAME
SORT OF GRACE YOU GIVE YOUR BABY
WHEN THEY FALL SHORT IN
THEIR FIRST ATTEMPT AT THINGS.
YOU'RE **BOTH** LEARNING
LOTS OF NEW
STUFF EVERY DAY.

FIND THE THING THAT
MAKES YOUR BABY LAUGH,
AND DO IT ALL THE TIME.
ONE MINUTE OF BABY BELLY LAUGHING
MAGICALLY ERASES ONE HOUR
OF NIGHT-CRYING EXHAUSTION.

THE BABY ENGINEERING
AND MANUFACTURING
PROCESS IS REMARKABLE.

THE ONLY PUZZLING PART IS
HOW THE OUTPUT CAN BE SO MUCH
GREATER THAN THE INPUT.

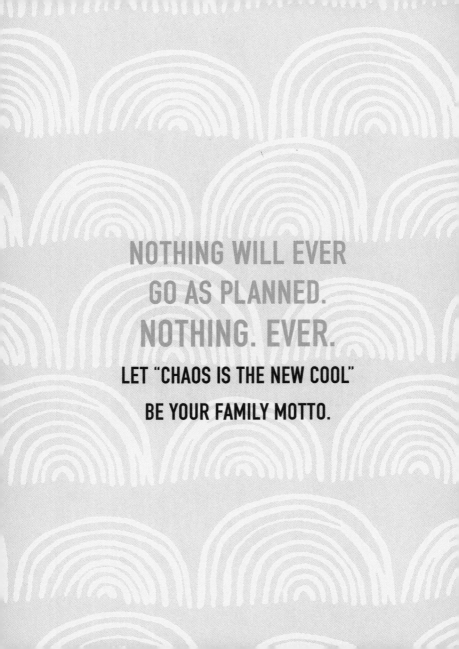

NOTHING WILL EVER
GO AS PLANNED.
NOTHING. EVER.

LET "CHAOS IS THE NEW COOL"

BE YOUR FAMILY MOTTO.

BE THE GENERATION TO BREAK THE "BIRTHDAY PARTY TREAT BAG" CURSE. THE ONLY REASON KIDS LEAVE PARTIES WITH A BAG OF DOODADS IS BECAUSE PARENTS AT LAST WEEK'S PARTY GAVE EVERYONE DOODADS.

**KEEP VIDEOS OF YOU
AND YOUR CHILD WHEN
THEY WERE A NEWBORN.**
**THEY NEED TO SEE
HOW YOU LOVED THEM
FROM THE VERY FIRST MOMENT
OF THEIR LIFE.**

FIND HOPE IN THIS:
THE IMPOSSIBLE CHALLENGES
OF TODAY WILL PASS.

(LONG PAUSE...)

THEY HAVE TO MAKE SPACE
FOR TOMORROW'S
IMPOSSIBLE CHALLENGES.

NOT EVERYTHING YOUR CHILD DOES NEEDS TO BE ON SOCIAL MEDIA.

THEY'RE CHILDREN, NOT INSTAGRAM PROPS.

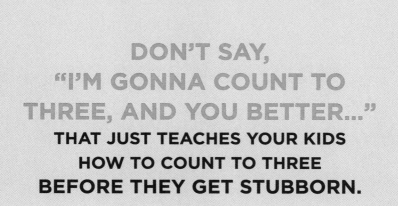

DON'T SAY,
"I'M GONNA COUNT TO
THREE, AND YOU BETTER..."
THAT JUST TEACHES YOUR KIDS
HOW TO COUNT TO THREE
BEFORE THEY GET STUBBORN.

NAP WHENEVER YOU CAN.

EVERY CHANCE YOU GET.

ALWAYS.

FOREVER.

SEE PREVIOUS:

IF YOUR CHILD IS SLEEPING
WHILE YOU'RE READING THIS,
PUT THE BOOK DOWN IMMEDIATELY
AND GO TO SLEEP.

FIND PARENTS WHO HAVE KIDS FIVE YEARS OLDER THAN YOURS. THEY HAVE TRAVELED DOWN THE PARENTING ROAD YOU'RE ON AND KNOW THE POTHOLES TO AVOID.

MAKE YOUR HOME "THE HOUSE"
WHERE KIDS HANG OUT.
IT'LL COST A SMALL FORTUNE
IN JUICE BOXES, POPSICLES, AND PIZZA,
BUT THE PROXIMITY TO YOUR KIDS AND
THEIR FRIENDS IS INVALUABLE.
(REMIND YOURSELF TO READ THIS
AGAIN WHEN THEY'RE 12.)

**DON'T EVER TRY
TO STOP SPEEDING VOMIT.
YOU'LL PUT
YOUR EYE OUT.**

LET YOUR CHILD
FALL ASLEEP ON YOUR CHEST
AS LONG AS YOU CAN.
YOU'LL KNOW IT'S TIME TO STOP
WHEN THEY CRUSH YOUR WINDPIPE.

HAVE FUN.

EVEN WITH ALL
THE STRESS AND EXHAUSTION
AND EXPENSE AND
SO MUCH PRIVATE-PART WIPING,
THERE'S FUN EVERY DAY.
MAKE SURE YOU FIND IT.

KEEP A JOURNAL OR
NOTEBOOK TO REMEMBER THE
FUN THINGS YOUR CHILD DOES.
IT WILL BE A TREASURE
TO YOU BOTH ONE DAY.

MAKE LOTS OF FUNNY FACES.
BABIES LOVE FUNNY FACES.
(AND THOSE OF US
WATCHING FROM ACROSS
THE ROOM LOVE THEM TOO.)

RESEARCH WOULD UNDOUBTEDLY
SHOW THAT 68.4% OF
A CHILD'S LIFETIME THROW-UPS
HAPPEN IN YEAR ONE.
ADMITTEDLY NOT GREAT NEWS
IF YOU HAVE A NEWBORN AT HOME, BUT
JUST IMAGINE HOW GREAT
THE MATH GETS AFTER THAT.

SOMETIMES YOU JUST
HAVE TO GENTLY
CLOSE THEIR BEDROOM DOOR,
WALK AWAY, AND LET THEM CRY.

IT'S HARD,
I KNOW.

GO ON VACATION AS
OFTEN AS YOU CAN.
"I REMEMBER WHEN WE..."
WILL BE ONE OF THE SWEETEST
PHRASES YOU HEAR WHEN YOUR
CHILDREN GET OLDER.

PRAY FOR YOUR KIDS DURING
THE GOOD TIMES AND THE HARD TIMES.
I REALIZED THE IMPORTANCE OF THIS WHILE
WALKING THROUGH A DARK HOUSE WITH
A FUSSY BABY AT 3:00 A.M.
(AT FIRST, I WAS MOSTLY PRAYING I WOULDN'T
SCREAM LOUDER THAN THE BABY.)

JUST SHOW UP.
PARENTING IS
NOT A SPECTATOR SPORT.
THE MOST IMPORTANT THING
YOU CAN DO IS TO
BE FULLY PRESENT IN
YOUR CHILD'S LIFE.

TELL YOUR KIDS
YOU LOVE THEM.
EVERY DAY.

ACTIONS ARE CERTAINLY IMPORTANT,
BUT WORDS SPEAK LIFE.

REMEMBER TRYING TO MERGE ONTO THE
INTERSTATE AFTER GETTING YOUR LEARNER'S PERMIT?
"THIS IS IMPOSSIBLE; I CAN'T DO IT."
BUT NOW YOU CAN CRUISE ALONG AT 70 WHILE
JUGGLING A BURGER, FRIES, AND A COKE.
PARENTING IS THE SAME.
"THIS IS IMPOSSIBLE; I CAN'T DO IT."
BUT THEN INSTINCTS SHARPEN,
CONFIDENCE GROWS, AND SOON YOU'RE
CHANGING A DIAPER WHILE FOLDING LEFTOVERS
AND PUTTING LAUNDRY IN THE MICROWAVE.

DRY HEAVES ARE NOT
A SIGN OF WEAKNESS.

BABY POOP AND
VOMIT REALLY ARE
JUST THAT SMELLY.

LET THEM MAKE MISTAKES.
IF THEY DON'T LEARN TO
SOLVE LITTLE PROBLEMS EARLY,
THEY WILL LIKELY HAVE TROUBLE
WITH BIG PROBLEMS LATER.

THINGS WILL NOT ALWAYS
GO THE WAY YOU PLANNED.
MANY TIMES, THEY WILL GO BETTER.
BUT SOMETIMES THEY GO
DUMPSTER-FIRE BAD.
WHEN THAT HAPPENS, YOUR JOB IS TO
BE FLEXIBLE AND RESILIENT ENOUGH
TO FIGHT YOUR WAY THROUGH.

JUST FOR FUN,
WHEN PEOPLE ASK,
"HOW OLD IS YOUR BABY?"
USE NUMBERS AND DECIMAL PLACES.
INSTEAD OF "SPARKY IS 19 MONTHS,"
SAY, "SPARKY IS 1.5833 YEARS."

WHEN YOUR CHILD IS LITTLE,
WHISPER ALL THE THINGS YOU
LOVE ABOUT THEM IN THEIR
TEENY, TINY EARS.
BECAUSE SOMETIME DOWN THE ROAD
(LIKE IN MIDDLE SCHOOL),
THEY WON'T LISTEN TO
A WORD YOU SAY.

SEE PREVIOUS:
THE SAME APPLIES
TO HOLDING HANDS.

JUST LIKE BABIES,
PARENTS CRY A LOT.
IT'S OKAY.
WE ALL DO IT.
BESIDES, MORE OFTEN THAN NOT,
YOU'LL BE HIDING IN THE CLOSET
WHERE NO ONE CAN SEE YOU.

WHEN YOUR CHILD
HAS AN EPIC MELTDOWN
IN THE MIDDLE OF A STORE,
REPEAT THIS
SIMPLE MANTRA TO YOURSELF:
"YOU WILL NEVER SEE
THESE PEOPLE AGAIN."

PARENTING IS A LOT LIKE
THE STOCK MARKET.
SOMETIMES YOU'RE UP,
SOMETIMES YOU'RE DOWN,
AND EVERY NOW AND THEN YOU'LL
HAVE A HORRIFIC CRASH.
BUT OVER TIME,
THINGS ALMOST
ALWAYS END UP POSITIVE.

NEVER COMPARE.
ANYTHING.
EVER.

DON'T LET SOCIAL EXPECTATIONS
BE THE BOSS OF YOU.
NEVER HAS SOMEONE SAID,
"I'M A FAILURE IN LIFE BECAUSE
MY PARENTS DIDN'T POST MY
SEVEN-MONTH PICTURE ON INSTA."

IT'S NOT FAIR TO PLACE EXPECTATIONS ON BABIES.

BESIDES, UNREALISTIC EXPECTATIONS WORK IN REVERSE: THE MORE YOU EXPECT, THE MORE LIKELY YOU ARE TO BE DISAPPOINTED.

THREE THINGS CAUSE
A BABY TO SCREAM:

1. BEING HUNGRY,

2. A DIRTY DIAPER, AND

3. BEING A BABY.

IT'S OKAY TO THINK

THE BABY IS SMILING AT YOU
WHEN MOST LIKELY THEY JUST
PASSED GAS OR DIRTIED A DIAPER.

YOU DESERVE ANY
SMILE YOU CAN GET.

MAKE UP SOME SILLY SONGS WITH SILLY VOICES.

MADE-UP WORDS WITH MADE-UP
MELODIES AND MADE-UP MOTIONS.
THE SILLIER AND LOUDER THE BETTER.
YOUR FAMILY WILL SING THESE SONGS FOREVER.

**BABIES ARE
SELFISH BECAUSE
THEY ARE BABIES.**

**PARENTS ARE SELFISH
JUST BECAUSE.
ONE MUST CHANGE.
GUESS WHICH ONE.**

PARENTING IS LIKE SITTING
ON THE SUPREME COURT:

YOU MUST BE MINDFUL OF PRECEDENTS.
YOU CAN'T DO MONTHLY PROGRESS PHOTOS
FOR CHILD NUMBER ONE AND THEN HAVE
NOTHING BETWEEN BIRTH AND SENIOR PROM
FOR CHILD NUMBER FOUR.

KIDS' MATH IS SIMPLE.

TIME = LOVE.

THERE IS NO SUBSTITUTE
FOR YOUR TIME
AND ATTENTION.

BE PATIENT ENOUGH
TO LET YOUR CHILD'S
PASSIONS COME TO THE SURFACE.
THEY WILL APPEAR;
THERE'S JUST NO WAY TO KNOW
WHEN OR WHY OR HOW.

JUST BECAUSE YOU LIKE SOMETHING
DOESN'T NECESSARILY MEAN YOUR
KIDS WILL. THAT'S OKAY;
MAYBE YOU WILL FIND
SOMETHING NEW TO LIKE.

HAVING A BABY IS
1% PINTEREST AND
99% PINTEREST FAIL.

**FRANKLY, THERE'S JUST AS MUCH
BEAUTY IN THE CHAOS AS THERE IS IN
THE SOFT FILTERS AND HAZY LIGHT.**

THE FINANCIAL AD DISCLAIMER
"PAST PERFORMANCE DOES NOT
INDICATE FUTURE PERFORMANCE"
ALSO APPLIES TO BABIES.
JUST BECAUSE SHE DID SOMETHING
ONE WAY FOR THE PAST MONTH IS
NO INDICATOR SHE WILL DO IT
THAT WAY NEXT MONTH.

PEEKABOO
IS THE UNIVERSAL
BABY LANGUAGE.

ONE OF THE TOUGHEST MOMENTS IN PARENTING IS WHEN YOU REALIZE THAT EVERYTHING YOU DO IS DESIGNED TO MAKE YOURSELF AND YOUR EFFORTS OBSOLETE.

THERE WILL BE A TIME WHEN YOUR TODDLER KNOWS ONLY TWO WORDS: "WHY" AND "NO."

THIS IS NOT A GOOD TIME. ANSWER AS MANY WHYS AS YOU CAN AND RESPOND APPROPRIATELY TO ALL THE NOES.

YOU MAY FEEL AS IF IT
WOULD BE IMPOSSIBLE TO BE
MORE TIRED THAN YOU ARE RIGHT NOW,
BUT IT'S NOT TRUE.
YOU'LL BE EVEN MORE TIRED A WEEK
OR A MONTH OR A YEAR FROM NOW.
YES, YOU'RE WHIPPED, BUT TAKE HEART—
AT LEAST YOU'RE NOT
THE MOST TIRED EVER.
YET.

WHEN YOUR CHILD ASKS
TO READ ONE MORE BOOK,
THEY REALLY MEAN
ONE HUNDRED MORE BOOKS.

YOUR PARENTING SHOULD
NOT BE DEFINED BY YOUR
SOCIAL MEDIA LIKES
BUT RATHER BY HOW
LIKEABLE YOUR CHILD IS.

YOU WON'T BE A PERFECT PARENT,
AND THAT'S OKAY.
YOUR PARENTS WEREN'T PERFECT,
AND YET HERE YOU ARE,
A MOSTLY RESPONSIBLE ADULT
CHARGED WITH THE
CARE AND NURTURE
OF A SMALL HUMAN BEING.

THERE ARE ZERO "NUGGET" FOODS

THAT NATURALLY OCCUR
IN THE WILD OR A GARDEN OR
A FARM OR THE SEA. DO WITH
THAT WHAT YOU WILL.

YOU ARE PARENTING
TO DEVELOP GOOD KIDS
WHO BECOME GREAT ADULTS.
THERE WILL ALWAYS BE SHORT-TERM
CHALLENGES TO ADDRESS, BUT REMEMBER
YOU'RE IN IT FOR THE LONG HAUL.

DO NOT PLACE YOUR IDENTITY
IN WHO YOUR KIDS ARE
OR WHAT THEY DO. THAT LIMITS YOU
AND IS NOT FAIR TO THEM.

NICKNAMES STICK.
BE CAREFUL
WHAT YOU CALL YOUR CHILDREN.
(FOR THE RECORD, THERE'S NEVER
BEEN A PRESIDENT STINKY
PANTS OR A NOBEL PRIZE WINNER
NAMED FUSSY FACE.)

IN THE SAME WAY,
BE CAREFUL WITH INITIALS.
BRANDON ULYSSES TYLER THOMAS
IS GONNA HAVE A HARD TIME ON THE PLAYGROUND,
AND SUSAN IRENE CATHERINE KENNEDY
WILL HEAR SOME SNICKERS WHEN WEARING
HER MONOGRAMMED DRESS.

YOU WILL CONTINUE BEING A PARENT LONG AFTER YOUR KIDS LEAVE HOME. WHEN TOUGH MOMENTS COME AND TEMPERS FLARE, DO ALL YOU CAN TO PROTECT THE RELATIONSHIP. FRUSTRATIONS WILL PASS, BUT RELATIONSHIPS LAST A LIFETIME.

PARENTING SOMETIMES FEELS
JUST THIS SIDE OF IMPOSSIBLE.
IT'S NOT;
IT JUST FEELS THAT WAY.

NEVER SAY

"IF YOU COULD ONLY BE LIKE
(ANOTHER CHILD)."
THAT IS A LIFE-SUCKING PHRASE.
DON'T BE A LIFE-SUCKING PARENT.

BE A LIFE-GIVING PARENT.
FIND THE WORDS OR ACTIONS
THAT HELP YOUR CHILDREN
FEEL BETTER ABOUT THEMSELVES.

WHEN YOUR CHILD SAYS,
"LOOK AT ME,"
THAT MEANS SOMETHING
IMPORTANT TO THEM IS HAPPENING.
THINGS THAT ARE IMPORTANT TO YOUR KIDS
SHOULD BE IMPORTANT TO YOU.

LET YOUR KIDS LOSE SOMETIMES
SO THEY LEARN THAT THINGS
WON'T ALWAYS GO THEIR WAY.
THIS DOESN'T MEAN YOU SHOULD
DO AN ENDZONE DANCE WHEN YOU
WIN HUNGRY HUNGRY HIPPOS,
BUT IT'S OKAY TO LET THEM LAND ON
THE DREADED CHUTES AND LADDERS
"BACK TO THE BEGINNING" SLIDE.

ALWAYS REMEMBER THAT FIRST
AND FOREMOST YOU ARE A PARENT.
YOU CAN BE A FRIEND OR A BUDDY
OR A PAL TOO. SOMETIMES.
BUT ALWAYS A PARENT.
MAKE DECISIONS ACCORDINGLY.

MASLOW'S HIERARCHY OF NEEDS
FOR NEW PARENTS:
SLEEP, DIAPERS, COFFEE.
SELF-PRESERVATION WILL TEMPORARILY
REPLACE SELF-ACTUALIZATION.

NEVER GIVE UP.
THE PAIN, HEARTACHE,
AND EXHAUSTION WILL PASS AWAY,
BUT THE LOVE WILL LAST FOREVER.
(OKAY, THAT'S NOT ENTIRELY TRUE.
THE EXHAUSTION NEVER REALLY ENDS.)

YOU'LL MAKE MISTAKES.
IT'S OKAY.
YOU'RE HUMAN.
THE MOST IMPORTANT THING
IS TO SAY "I'M SORRY."
QUICKLY. MISTAKES PASS;
HUMILITY LASTS.

DON'T WORRY WHAT
THE HOUSE LOOKS LIKE.
YOU'VE GOT LIMITED TIME
AND ENERGY. KID FIRST. YOU
AND SPOUSE A CLOSE SECOND.
PINTEREST-PERFECT HOUSE IS A
DISTANT NINTH.

QUESTION:

HOW MANY TIMES HAVE YOU HEARD THIS? "MY CHILDHOOD WOULD HAVE BEEN SO MUCH BETTER IF OUR HOUSE WAS CLEANER."

ANSWER:

ZERO TIMES. NOBODY SAYS THAT. NEITHER WILL YOUR KIDS. THEY WON'T REMEMBER HOW CLEAN THE HOUSE WAS, BUT THEY WILL REMEMBER THE TIME YOU HAD A SLEEPOVER IN THE FORT YOU BUILT IN THE DEN.

IMPORTANT SCIENCE FACT:
BABY VOMIT IS NOT BOUND BY THE
LAWS OF PHYSICS. IT CAN CHANGE FORM,
DIRECTION, COLOR, CONSISTENCY,
AND VELOCITY AS IT DESIRES.

SAVE VIDEOS.

AND NOT JUST BIRTHDAY PARTIES OR HOME RUNS OR DANCE RECITALS. EVERYDAY LIFE TOO. READING BOOKS. TALKING IN THE CAR. LONGER ONES THAT INCLUDE WHOLE CONVERSATIONS ARE TREASURES.

DON'T MAKE EMPTY THREATS.

IF YOU SAY YOU'RE GOING
TO DISCIPLINE, DO IT.
IF YOU'RE NOT,
DON'T SAY IT.

USE TIME IN THE
CAR TO TALK.
KIDS STRAPPED INTO
A FIVE-POINT HARNESS
ARE A CAPTIVE AUDIENCE.

BUY AN
INDUSTRIAL-STRENGTH
CARPET CLEANER.
AND A BACKUP.
NO FURTHER INSTRUCTION NEEDED.

IT'S OKAY
(AND FRANKLY, VERY HEALTHY)
TO ASK FOR HELP.

DON'T SET AN UNSUSTAINABLE NURSERY PRECEDENT.

IT'S INCREDIBLY AWKWARD WHEN BABY SISTER DISCOVERS BIG SISTER HAD A SUPER ELABORATE DESIGNER SUITE, BUT BABY SISTER SPENT HER FIRST SIX MONTHS SLEEPING IN A HAND-ME-DOWN CRIB IN HER PARENTS' BEDROOM CLOSET.

**SHARE RITUALS
WITH YOUR CHILD.**
THEY DON'T NEED TO BE BIG
("ON SATURDAYS, SPARKY
AND I REPAINT THE GARAGE").
IN FACT, SMALLER IS BETTER
("ON SATURDAYS, SPARKY AND I STOP
AT THE MARKET AND GET A COKE").
RITUALS BRING COMFORT.

YOU WILL HAVE TO MAKE SOME
DIFFICULT TIME-MANAGEMENT DECISIONS.
THINGS THAT WERE IMPORTANT PRE-BABY
WILL LIKELY BECOME LESS IMPORTANT.
YOU CAN ALWAYS GET BACK YOUR
GOLF SWING OR TAKE A SHOPPING TRIP.
YOU CAN'T GET BACK THE
TIME YOU MISSED WITH YOUR KIDS.

TRY TO BE CONSISTENT,
NOT PERFECT.

ASK YOUR PARENTS FOR ADVICE.

SURE, THEY DROVE YOU CRAZY,
BUT THEY MUST HAVE DONE
SOME THINGS RIGHT TO
GET YOU TO THIS POINT.

DO WHAT'S RIGHT
FOR YOUR CHILD,
NOT FOR FACEBOOK OR INSTAGRAM.
DON'T TRY TO CONVINCE THE WORLD
YOUR LIFE IS PERFECT JUST BECAUSE
THAT JERK FROM HIGH SCHOOL
HAS AN AMAZING FEED.

MAKING ACTIVITIES
A ZERO-SUM GAME
BRINGS SOME SANITY.

WHEN SOMETHING IS ADDED TO THE
FAMILY CALENDAR (A SPORTS PRACTICE,
A CHURCH COMMITMENT, A SLEEPOVER),
SOMETHING MUST BE SUBTRACTED.

IT'S OKAY TO PERIODICALLY WALK
(OR RUN IF NECESSARY)
AWAY FROM A SCREAMING BABY. (BUT NOT ALL THE TIME, AND NOT ALL THE WAY ACROSS TOWN.)

HERE'S MY NONSCIENTIFIC
ADVICE ON YOUR KID'S MILESTONES:

DON'T STRESS AND DON'T FREAK OUT.
SOMETIMES YOUR CHILD WILL BE AHEAD,
AND SOMETIMES THEY'LL BE BEHIND.
MORE OFTEN THAN NOT, IT EVENS OUT.
MORE IMPORTANTLY,
IT DOESN'T REALLY MATTER EITHER WAY.

LAY ON THE FLOOR
TO SEE THINGS THE WAY
YOUR BABY DOES.
REGARDLESS OF HOW OLD
YOUR CHILD IS,
IT HELPS TO GET
THEIR PERSPECTIVE.

LIFE HACK:

**USE BABY GIGGLES FOR
YOUR ALARM RING TONE
TO MAGICALLY ERASE THE
WAILING IN YOUR HEAD FROM
THE NIGHT BEFORE.**

PROUD GRANDDAD

REMEMBER HOW GRANDPA SAID THIS?
"WHEN I WAS LITTLE, WE DIDN'T HAVE FANCY
TOYS. WE HAD STICKS AND A BOX. OUR TOYS
DIDN'T LIGHT UP AND BEEP AND MAGICALLY
BECOME OTHER TOYS. IF WE WANTED A TOY TO
BECOME A DIFFERENT TOY,
WE JUST BROKE OUR STICK IN HALF."
YEAH, THAT'S PROBABLY NOT EXACTLY RIGHT,
BUT THERE IS TRUTH TO THE IDEA
THAT SIMPLER IS BETTER.

BATH TIME IS 99.9%
AWESOMENESS FILLED
WITH GIGGLES
AND BUBBLES AND SMILES.
THE OTHER .1% IS
WRASSLIN' A SLIPPERY EEL.
BUT HERE'S THE GOOD NEWS—
ALL THAT WATER SPLASHED OUT OF THE TUB
WILL DRY BEFORE BATH TIME TOMORROW.

YOU LOVE YOUR
LITTLE ONE MORE
THAN YOU KNEW WAS POSSIBLE.
LET THEM KNOW THAT
EVERY DAY.

PARENTING IS ALL ABOUT
MANAGING RISK.
WHEN YOUR CHILD
GRABS FOOD OFF THE FLOOR,
THE MOST IMPORTANT QUESTION ISN'T
"DID THE DOG LICK THAT FOOD?"
BUT RATHER
"WHAT DID THE DOG LICK
BEFORE HE LICKED THAT FOOD?"

THERE IS NO AVERAGE CHILD.

THERE IS NO MEDIAN OR REGULAR KID. EVERY CHILD HAS THEIR OWN SPECIAL AND UNIQUE STRENGTHS AND WEAKNESSES. YOUR JOB IS TO HELP THEM FIND THEIR STRENGTHS OR DESIRES AND GUIDE THEM TOWARD THOSE.

EVER HAD A FRIEND SAY THIS?

"MY SPARKY'S AMAZING. COACH SAID SHE'S
THE BEST THREE-YEAR-OLD BUMBLEBEE LEAGUE
SOCCER PLAYER HE'S SEEN. OLYMPICS OR BUST."
HANG ON NOW; LET'S PUMP THE BRAKES.
THE MORE (AND I THINK, THE EARLIER) WE PUSH A
CHILD IN A DIRECTION, THE GREATER THE RISK OF THEM
FEELING TRAPPED DOING SOMETHING THEY DON'T LOVE.
OR THE MORE LIKELY THEY ARE TO BURN OUT
BEFORE MIDDLE SCHOOL.
BOTH ARE BAD.

DON'T FORCE A NICKNAME
ON YOUR CHILD.
THE BEST NICKNAMES
COME NATURALLY,
BORN OUT OF EXPERIENCES
OR THE LOVE OF FAMILY.

KEEP AN EMERGENCY KIT

IN EVERY ROOM OF THE HOUSE.
THESE KITS SHOULD CONTAIN
DIAPERS, WIPES, AND CHOCOLATE.

GRANDPAS ARE UNFLAPPABLE,
LIKE THOSE CARTOON CHARACTERS CASUALLY
WALKING OUT OF EXPLODING BUILDINGS AND
SWEEPING THE DUST OFF THEIR SHOULDERS.
UNFLAPPABLENESS CAN'T BE BOUGHT OR
DOWNLOADED OR BORROWED.
IT'S THE RESULT OF DECADES
OF FRONT-LINE PARENTING.
LEARN FROM THEM.

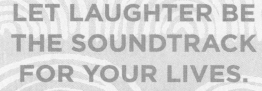

LET LAUGHTER BE
THE SOUNDTRACK
FOR YOUR LIVES.
LAUGH WHEN YOUR CHILD IS FUNNY,
LAUGH WHEN THEY LAUGH,
AND WHEN YOU CAN, LAUGH AT
THE CHAOS LIFE BRINGS YOU.

WHEN YOU'RE HAVING
ONE OF THOSE DAYS WHEN YOUR
BABY WON'T STOP SPITTING UP AND
YOU WANT TO GIVE UP,
JUST REMEMBER—YOUR PARENTS
HAD THE SAME DAYS RAISING YOU.
BUT WITHOUT DISNEY+.

THE MOST IMPORTANT THING
YOU CAN DO FOR YOUR BABY IS
PRAY FOR THEM.
PRAY WHEN YOU ARE SNUGGLING.
PRAY WHEN YOU ARE WALKING.
PRAY WHEN YOU ARE NURSING OR
FEEDING OR BATHING OR BOUNCING.
PRAY WHEN YOU ARE HAPPY.
PRAY WHEN YOU ARE FRUSTRATED.
PRAY WHEN YOU ARE TUCKING IN OR
PICKING UP OR CORRECTING OR KISSING.
PRAY ALL THE TIME.